WE ALWAYS...

MAKING MEMORIES
THAT LAST A LIFETIME

This book is dedicated to each and every one of our faithful and generous Partners. We couldn't do this work without you.

Acknowledgements

As always, it has taken a great team of people to see this book become a reality. A massive thanks goes to Jess Hills for all her hard work in project managing this book. Thanks also to Esther Holt, Sarah Rowlands, Stephen Hayes, Claire Burton and our brilliant PA, Jody Jones. Finally, we are so grateful to our wonderful Partners and friends of Care for the Family and the many other families who have shared their treasured traditions with us, without whom this book would not have been written.

A friend once told me (Rob) that as a child they used to buy a patch as a souvenir every time they went on holiday. Each of those patches told a story and held a memory of time together as a family. The patches theme throughout this book is a simple nod to that tradition and a reminder that our memories last far longer than the few hours or days they take to create.

CONTENTS

INTRODUCTION

Over the years, Dianne and I have had the opportunity of talking with thousands of people about their childhoods, and time and again, those who described their families as strong and loving also spoke of their cherished family traditions. Whether these families were rich or poor, from the country or the inner city, were headed by two parents or a single parent, and whatever their cultural background, their responses were often the same. When asked what made the memories of their family life sweet, sooner or later they'd start a sentence with, "We always ..."

In writing this book, we asked as many people as possible to share with us their favourite family traditions. What you'll read in the pages to come is a compilation of those treasured times. The traditions people have shared with us have been many and varied. They are often to do with special days of the year. One family said they always light candles on Christmas Eve and watch It's *A Wonderful Life*. Another family always go for a walk in a busy park on Boxing Day, and as people come towards them, they try to guess what presents they are wearing! One family sings "Auld Lang Syne" holding hands together in the street outside their home on New Year's Eve, and they then have a curry afterwards, sharing hopes and dreams for the year ahead around the table.

We often think back to traditions we had when our children were young. A big one for us was 'Family Night.' Once a week the kids would drag their mattresses across the landing and sleep on our bedroom floor. And once a month we would have a 'Super Family Night'. This was a little more complicated and involved us all dragging our mattresses downstairs and sleeping on the living room floor. Now there's no good reason why four people with perfectly good beds upstairs should want to do that – except that it's fun. We'd light the fire, eat chocolate and tell stories in the darkness.

We used to talk about that tradition in our seminars and books, and we were once confronted by a man who initially seemed not too impressed with our suggestion.

He said, "I have four kids and we tried the whole 'Super Family Night' thing. You know – beds downstairs, stories in the dark and eating chocolate." We nodded nervously. He went on, "Three of my kids were sick all over their mattresses and the fourth threw up in my wife's car the next day." Then a huge smile crossed his face and he said, "It was worth it, though. Thanks for the memory."

We have often thought about what he said: how the silliness, the hassle – even scraping the sick from the back seat of the Volvo – was worth it. Don't despise traditions. Whether they are simple or profound, traditions say to us, "You belong here – these are your roots."

Traditions are not always easy. For those who are bereaved, traditions can be painful and challenging to navigate. We will never forget the loved ones that are no longer with us and there are many ways that we can remember them by including them in our traditions as the years pass. This might involve looking at treasured photo albums, visiting their favourite places or perhaps, like one family, having a special bauble to represent them on the Christmas tree.

But it's not just in bereavement that traditions can be challenging. One mother told us how she tackled bringing together quite different Christmas traditions in her blended family:

> I brought my three children with me to live with my new husband and his two sons. As we discussed preparations for our first Christmas together, we realised we had different traditions, so we decided to create some new ones. My youngest child went to choose the Christmas tree together with his new stepdad, which has happened every year since then. But it wasn't all so easy. His children were used to having stockings at the end of their beds on Christmas morning, which they could open as soon as

they awoke. My children had to wait and always had everything downstairs. We added these traditions together so they all had stockings by their beds with smaller presents in and then had larger presents in the lounge, which we opened together. Everyone was pleased!

Don't feel pressurised into copying other families; when we do that, it's not long before our joy is robbed from us. One size doesn't fit all, and what's important is that your traditions work for your family. And if plans become too complicated or unachievable, then change them – they are yours to make or to lay aside. There are many reasons why traditions come to an end. While it can be something definitive that changes a tradition, such as the addition of a new family member, marriage, the loss of a loved one, or a house move, it could be that a tradition has simply run its course; they don't need to last forever.

The family acts as a bulwark against the storms of life. It should be a place of training, security and safety, but it also has another vital function. It gives us a sense of identity; it helps us know our place in the world – perhaps even the universe. Traditions help in that. They create a sense of connectedness. They say 'This is the way we do things around here. This is where I belong.'

You may have treasured traditions from your own cultural background that are not mentioned in this book. Your heritage can bring a rich flavour and uniqueness to your family traditions. Why not experiment with some that we've suggested by adding your own cultural references to them? Who knows – the ones that you begin now may be passed down through many generations in years to come.

If you're looking to be intentional with your family traditions but aren't sure where to start, here are some pointers that may help:

- Be ready to start new traditions, whether that be through meticulous planning or spontaneously.
- Be willing to tweak or abandon any traditions that no longer work for you. You may have outgrown some traditions and that's OK.
- Find out whether there are any family traditions from previous generations that you could adapt and carry on.
- Pick one from this book to try.
- Have fun!

We don't want this book to remain in perfect condition, gathering dust on a bookshelf. Our hope is that it's packed in holiday suitcases, brought out on dark winter evenings, taken on long car journeys and becomes a part of daily life. We hope that it will be used by families, by grandparents, by couples and by friends. We want its pages to become dog-eared and stained with the memories of your own traditions. But perhaps most of all, we hope that many years from now when somebody asks an older person in your family what they remember most about their family life, that they will smile and say, "Oh, we always ..."

EVERYDAY TRADITIONS

It's likely that we have all come across friends and family who have traditions that are specific to them and their loved ones. Some of these may seem lavish and unachievable to us! The level of detail involved may sound intricate and overwhelming, not to mention how much they may cost in money, time and energy. In fact, hearing of some traditions may fill us with a sense of dismay that makes us run in the opposite direction – they just feel like too much to undertake. The well-known phrase 'comparison is the thief of joy' extends to traditions too. Our family traditions are just that – our family traditions!

Comparing what we do as a family to what another family is doing will only rob us of the joy that our own traditions and memories bring. It can be great to use what another family is doing as inspiration and ideas for what we could also do, but being competitive or comparing ourselves to others doesn't build us up as a family – it only creates envy and disappointment. If you enjoy elaborate traditions and find joy and purpose in planning every little detail, then please keep making those precious memories with your family. But if you're feeling under pressure to come up with the most unique way to kick-start your weekend, don't worry – there are plenty of ideas in the pages to come, and you can put your own spin on them.

Every family is unique and when it comes to making memories and family traditions, anything goes. You may have picked up this book feeling as though you can't think of a single tradition that you had as a child, or can share with your family now. We would bet that, in fact, you can. You see, there may well be things that you do as a family that are so embedded in your daily life that you haven't even realised are traditions. Remember, traditions are customs or rituals that families do over and over again, which can encompass anything from reading stories at bedtime to always making ice cream sundaes on a Friday night and everything in between.

The movie and popcorn nights that you hold on the first day of the school holidays may have become so normalised that you don't realise they are established traditions that your children may fondly recall to their grandchildren one day. The late-night car journeys to pick up fish and chips on a Friday night may have become so routine that you've forgotten this isn't something that every family does. Why not take some time to think about the routines and activities, both day-to-day and special, that you do as a family? If you have children, why not involve them in the conversation too? Children often see the world in different ways to how we see it as adults and you may be amazed at the family routines, rituals and traditions that your children can identify.

In this first section, you'll find stories about everyday traditions. Many of these activities and rituals take very little money or time, and yet they have left such an impact on the lives of the people that have shared them with us. There is no doubt in our minds that there was a twinkle in their eyes when they wrote them down. From talking about the highs and lows of each day to roasting marshmallows and den-making, this first section is all about traditions that happen regularly and have become a part of daily life.

> We always say a special little poem and then an ancient blessing before bedtime.
>
> **CHARLOTTE**

> My dad always makes tea on a little gas stove whenever we go out for family walks – and we do go on long Saturday walks a lot, something that we've carried on from my childhood.
>
> We also often have our picnic out of the back of the family car, once leading my oldest brother to complain that we never sat at a picnic table like a normal family!
>
> SARA

We love creating traditions and making memories with our grandkids. Whenever they come for a sleepover at our home, we always make pancakes together and take turns flipping them. We line up all of our toppings: maple syrup, lemon and sugar and chocolate spread, so that everything is ready and nothing delays us filling our hot pancakes straight from the pan.

This tradition, and the many others that we share, not only create special memories but also help to build a great connection with our grandkids. We laugh and play together right from the moment that they wake up – even if that means that our day begins at 5.50 am due to some very excited children!

Our time together is very bonding and when it comes to the pancakes, they're also learning new skills.

CAROLINE

We always talk about our
'high and low' of the day when
we eat dinner together.

LAWRENCE

Every Friday, my dad would let one of us kids make the sandwich that he would take to work for lunch. Needless to say, the chocolate spread and Wotsit crisp sandwich that I made wasn't his favourite!

This tradition with my dad was something that made a personal connection with him and it also encouraged conversation with him when he got home from work, as we would love hearing what he thought of our sandwich.

LUKE J

IDEAS FOR TRADITIONS INVOLVING FOOD

1. Have a meal together with no devices

2. Design and make your own ice cream sundaes

3. Invite another family over for food on a particular day of the month

4. Cook food from a culture different to yours (this could be a different culture each time)

5. Eat your favourite sweets on a Friday afternoon when school has finished

"

A favourite tradition
of mine is Friday pizza night.
Sometimes it's just the four of us, but
often we invite others and they join in
with the tradition. Our kids love pizza
and my husband is a fabulous cook, so
those two things make it really special.
And for me, it is also the marking of
the end of the week and the
beginning of a weekend.

GILL

"

For as long as I can remember, every Friday night my whole family gets together, including all of my aunts, uncles, cousins and grandparents that live locally. The house is crammed full of people and it's definitely not a night for peace and quiet!

We always eat a meal together and it's not just any meal. My mum is the most amazing cook and so it's always three courses of the best starters, main courses and desserts that you could imagine. It's no coincidence that it's my favourite meal of the week!

This is one of our most loved family traditions and something that I will definitely be passing on to my own children one day.

SAMUEL

> Once a month, we would
> hold a Celebration Breakfast when
> the kids were aged between three and
> twelve. We would have lots of lovely
> food and look back on the month and
> give thanks for anything and
> anyone we could think of.
>
> **ROBIN**

I have so many special memories of the traditions that we had growing up. One of my favourites is when the extended family would get together at my grandma's house on a Sunday at tea time for salmon sandwiches, cakes and crisps. There would be kids and adults in every corner of every room and as a child it was always something that I looked forward to.

I also remember that we would always buy a 10p mix of sweets walking home from primary school on a Friday. Then there was my mum's version of a well-known hot chicken sandwich that we would always eat after school on a Wednesday. We were even allowed to eat it in front of the TV which was such a treat.

They were all really enjoyable moments and time put aside to do things with other family members. They were also special because they brought structure to our week, as we knew we had these things to look forward to come rain or shine.

CLAIRE

Having breakfast in bed on the weekends was one of my favourite family traditions as a child. We would all run into Mum and Dad's room and jump on their bed before Dad got up and made us all breakfast. It was always such a treat and we were all together, which made it even more special.

VANESSA

Every Sunday evening, we make cheese and ham toasties and eat them on the sofa in front of a film. It's such a nice end to the weekend and a chance to all be together.

We normally eat supper at the kitchen table, and so eating our toasties on the sofa is a change of routine and something that we all really look forward to. It's also so nice to not have to do any 'real cooking' on a Sunday night. I get the machine out and everyone picks what they want in their toasties. One of my daughters particularly likes the bread for her toastie to be buttered on the outside too and will often remind me to do that! Once the food is ready, we'll all sit down together and watch a film or TV programme.

It's an opportunity to spend quality time together, eat comforting food and recharge before the week ahead. I would choose this over anything else on a Sunday evening!

KATE

We have many traditions in our family, but one of favourites is to play what we call 'The flour game'. We excitedly fill a bowl with flour, pack it down and continue to do this until the bowl is full to top. We then level it off, place a plate over the bowl, carefully tip it upside-down and lift the bowl off, creating a mound of flour on the plate. We place a cherry on top of our flour mound, and that's when the fun really begins!

We each take it in turns to carefully cut the flour, using a butter knife, while trying to make sure that the cherry doesn't fall off. Slowly but surely, the flour mound gets leaner and leaner until all that's left is a very narrow tower with a cherry balancing precariously on its top. The cutting of this flour tower cautiously continues until the cherry dramatically falls. And how does that cherry need to be retrieved by the person who caused it to topple? By using only their mouth, of course!

At least one of us ends up covered in flour while everyone else is in fits of laughter. It's such a great family game that everyone can get involved with and it brings us a lot of joy!

LLOYD

IDEAS FOR
TRADITIONS AT THE WEEKENDS

1. Have breakfast in bed

2. Do a device-free activity together

3. Have a pyjama morning

4. Have a regular Saturday morning family activity, for example swimming

5. Hold family board game nights

We always have the extended family to our house for dinner on special occasions.

KATIE

66 As a child, I loved our
tradition of stopping at the chip
shop after swimming on Saturday and
eating our food in the car. My younger
brother would accidentally drop
his chips in the footwell every time,
exasperating my mum hugely! 99

CAMILLA

AFTER-SWIMMING CHIPS

We have a tradition that we call 'Rabbits' that was passed down from my grandma. On the first of every month, the first person to announce 'Rabbits' would win!

Years on, my mum, my brother and I have taken on this tradition and still do it to this day (my brother and I are in our thirties and moved out of our mum's home many years ago). We have a family WhatsApp group just for the three of us and the first person to write RABBITS in the group chat, on the first of each month, wins that month's point. We often all stay up until 00:00:01 to be the first to write it and it has become incredibly competitive. We have rules that forbid alarms, reminders or help from spouses and we even keep a tally of who has won each month. A few years ago, we bought a wooden statue of two rabbits dancing as a prize for the winner. This statue now moves from house to house each year depending on who the overall winner for the year is.

It's special to us as it's something that only we do. It brings us a lot of joy and laughter and has created such great memories. It brings us together via technology, when in reality we're miles apart.

JESS

> We always have a sleepover in the living room on the first weekend back in school after a holiday. It's something for our girls to look forward to, knowing that it will happen.
>
> **CLAIRE**

Since the pandemic we go on a regular walk with our friends and children. We take camping kettles in our rucksacks with us and when we've made it over the top of the hill and down into the woods, we make a small fire, boil the kettles and have hot drinks and biscuits. Sometimes we will roast marshmallows and the kids will make a den too.

PAUL

IDEAS FOR OUTDOOR TRADITIONS

1. Build a den when out with family friends

2. Make daisy chains for each other and press the flowers

3. Organise a nature hunt in a new place each time

4. Light a fire pit and toast marshmallows (disposable barbecues work well too!)

5. Have a picnic – each person gets to choose one item to take

"Most Saturdays, as teenagers, we would have a special 'picky' lunch. My mum would drive to the local supermarket to pick up a freshly baked baguette and we would each choose our favourite fillings to go with it. It was such a simple thing to do, but almost thirty years on I still look back at those special Saturday lunches with such fond memories."

ADAM

I was born in the UK to Kenyan parents and it's really important to me that, despite living in England, my children are brought up with an awareness of and appreciation for Kenyan traditions.

There are many traditions that we are passing on to them, but my favourite is our monthly culture nights where we cook traditional Kenyan food, play games that my parents played as children and wear traditional Kenyan dress.

KIONI

> As the kids got older and were in the teenager years, we used to always have Co-op chocolate milk and shared a bag of Squashies on a Sunday night. We had small milk bottles to drink from and these perfectly divided the drink between us all.
>
> We did this for about five years before Co-op changed the flavour and killed the tradition.
>
> **ROBIN**

One Christmas, we were given a fantastic family gift – a height chart that compares how tall you are to things such as a post box, different animals or famous people. We stuck it on our kitchen wall and it has been a huge hit.

Every six months, in January and July, the kids get measured and it's known in our house as 'The Big Measure'! Anyone who comes over to visit now has to be measured and written on there too.

KEREN

HEIGHT CHARTS FOR ALL

When I was young, we had
a tradition of eating pancakes on
a Friday night around the TV as a
family. Pancakes were a bit of a treat,
and we watched comedy shows,
so I remember laughing a lot.

GILL

As children, on a Sunday, we were always given the job of making the Sunday dinner table look amazing. I loved the tradition as it made me feel special. The humble dinner table suddenly became a fancy table in an exclusive restaurant. We could eat there every week, even if we couldn't afford it in real life!

The food was the glue that held it all together. It would always be something more special than everyday meals. Even if it was a simple lasagne, my mum would try and present it differently, like giving us each our own individual one. The special glasses and cutlery were used and we could choose the tablecloth too.

As an adult, I have now recreated this with my family, by having a Saturday 'family feast' where we make something special, taking time to choose and plan it and all coming together to eat.

ELISABETH

IDEAS FOR
BUDGET-FRIENDLY TRADITIONS

1. Volunteer on a community project together

2. Make a gratitude jar, by each writing down one thing that you're grateful for on a piece of paper and placing it inside. Do this until the jar is full and then empty it together, reading aloud all the things that you're grateful for

3. Cook a meal together on certain days

4. Make memories on the beach or in a local park

5. Have a treasure hunt in your garden or local area. Why not get your neighbours involved too?

When I was a teenager, Sunday lunch would be served at 1 pm on the dot, without exception. My mother would be cooking all morning, while my father would be playing golf at the local club. He would return just in time to stir the gravy (to him, he had made it) and then lunch could take place. I have such fond memories of this, even though it was many years ago.

NEIL

Use these pages to write or draw your own traditions.

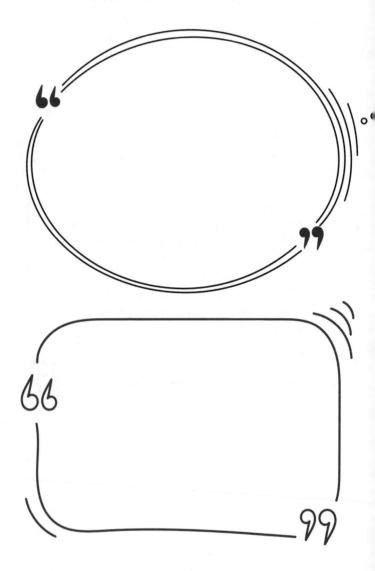

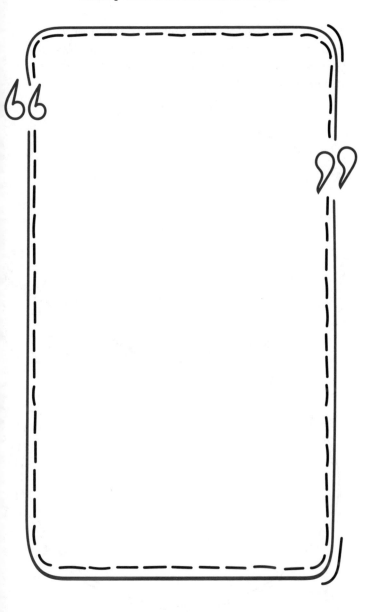

These pages are for you to fill with your memories. You may wish to use the space to write or draw your memories or stick in photos or memorabilia – the choice is yours!

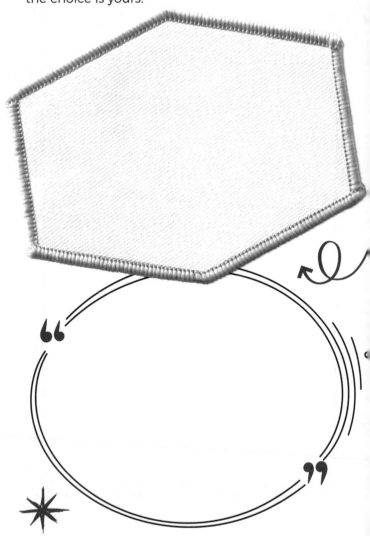

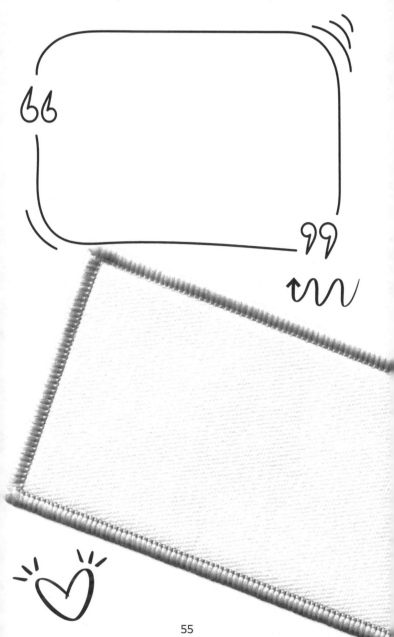

SEASONAL TRADITIONS

For many of us, when we hear the word 'tradition', we immediately think of Christmas. It's almost as if we can't have one without the other. Christmas is a season that is well known for quality time with family and making memories together. But seasonal traditions can be about so much more than just Christmas. When it comes to seasonal traditions, the clue is in the name! They are traditions that take place at certain times during the year, often dictated by the season. For example, Christmas always happens during the winter in the UK (or during the summer months if you live in Australia!) and Bonfire Night is the same date every November.

Seasonal traditions can include faith-based celebrations such as Easter, activities that revolve around the clocks going forwards or backwards or even how we see in each new year. Where you live can also impact the seasonal traditions that you have as a family. The UK has four nations, each of which has its own national holiday – St Patrick's Day, St Andrew's Day, St George's Day and St David's Day. All of these national holidays bring with them a whole host of traditions ranging from what is worn of those days to what is eaten in celebration. Each of these days is steeped in history and is special to its country. At these times, many people take the time to follow the traditions set by many generations before them. You and your family may well do some of them! Several areas of the UK are known for having their own local traditions too, such as cheese rolling, which hails from Gloucestershire and involves a nine-pound round of cheese being rolled from the top of a steep hill and competitors chasing after it! Why not find out if your local area has any special traditions that you and your family can get involved in?

There may also be seasonal traditions that are unique to you, ones which you have created to mark certain times of the year. From celebrating the first flower that blossoms in your garden in springtime to dancing outside during the first snowfall of the winter, there is no end to the possibilities that come with seasonal traditions. The only limit is our imagination!

In this next section, you'll find a whole host of seasonal traditions. Why not add your own too?

" We go to a pumpkin patch as a family every autumn. We choose some pumpkins that we'll later carve and decorate together, and then head to Starbucks for a Pumpkin Spice Latte. "

JORDAN

"

I'm single and live with some friends, so we get how hard it can be at Christmas when everyone is doing family or couple stuff. So, every year we throw our own Christmas party, which has become one of my favourite traditions.

This always takes place during December and everyone we know who lives alone, doesn't have family close by or is having a hard time is invited. I love this evening as it brings people together and no one is left out.

ABI

"

I grew up in America and we had many traditions throughout the year. One of these traditions was to always decorate the house for Thanksgiving together as a family. We would also celebrate this holiday season together too.

There is a department store in America named Macy's and every year it presents an annual Thanksgiving Day parade in New York City. It's a three-hour televised parade which ends at Macy's department store in Manhattan and if you're lucky enough to be in New York City when it takes place, you can stand and watch the parade go by. The parade is made up of balloons and floats and features live music and other performances from acts such as choirs, marching bands, cheerleaders and dancers.

One of our traditions was to always watch the Macy's parade on the TV while cooking Thanksgiving dinner. It was also a tradition to make my grandfather's delicious homemade stuffing. I made sure to continue these traditions with my children, even though Thanksgiving isn't celebrated in the UK. It was important to me that my children learnt about their American heritage and having these traditions encouraged this.

KAT

> We always hide chocolate eggs in our garden for our children to find. There is such delight in their faces as they run around looking for the special eggs that the 'Easter bunny' has left for them. Some people may say that they're getting a bit too old for chocolate egg hunts but they passionately disagree!

VICTORIA

We had a tradition in our family whereby we would wake our kids up at 2 am one morning close to Christmas and take them to our local supermarket to do the festive food shop. They absolutely loved it! Our son cannot wait to do the same with his boys when they are a little older.

SIAN

IDEAS FOR
BONFIRE NIGHT TRADITIONS

1. Special hot chocolates with marshmallows and cream

2. Buy sparklers for your neighbours and watch the local fireworks together

3. Eat the same meal every year, for example hotdogs or chilli

4. Wrap up warm and attend a local bonfire, or safely make your own

5. Have a craft evening with a Bonfire Night theme

> We always go and watch the World Conker Championships which are held on the second Sunday of October. One year, we happened to be in the local area at the time that they're held and we've been going back to watch it ever since – even though it's a four-hour drive! We take notes on the techniques that the players use and then hold our own competitions when we get home!

SARAH

"
Every year, as a family,
each person shares about a
song that has been especially
poignant or special to us
throughout that year. Then we play
them all and reflect on the
last twelve months.
"

BETH

We're a bit Tolkien-obsessed in my family, and my dad decided to incorporate two of Tolkien's characters, the dwarves Gimli and Gloin, into our Christmas traditions. Basically, Father Christmas didn't have elves to help him make presents, but dwarves. They would make all the presents and then drop them off for Father Christmas to pick them up on Christmas Eve.

Growing up, we lived near a river and you could see it from our window, and this is where Gimli and Gloin would leave our presents for Father Christmas, for obviously they travelled from the North Pole by boat! This would only happen if my dad gave the dwarves the 'Dwarf Call'. This consisted of my dad standing in the front garden, putting his thumbs on his nose with his palms facing out and bellowing a loud, "AAAWOOOOOooooo!" This let the dwarves know that we'd been good that year and they could leave the presents. We would then excitedly race to bed, knowing our presents were being handed safely over to Father Christmas.

It's such a unique tradition and it shows how much my dad enjoyed playing with us and encouraging our imaginations. When we looked at the twinkling lights dancing on the river, we genuinely believed we could 'see' Gimli and Gloin in their little boat. I love that!

LUKE M

We always celebrate Hogmanay with our neighbours. My parents are Scottish and while we don't live in Scotland anymore, we still celebrate Hogmanay as it's part of our heritage.

Some of the traditions that we have – such as giving gifts – are associated with Hogmanay across Scotland, while others – such as always ending the evening with a conga line – have been made up by us!

JOEL

Despite no longer living in India, we still make every effort to celebrate Indian festivals throughout the year.

While what we're able to do in the UK looks very different to what we would be doing in India (where the entire community would come together and celebrations would often last until the early hours of the morning), it's still an important part of our culture as a family. For us, celebrations often involve cooking traditional recipes, decorating our home and gathering together to enjoy some fireworks.

SHIVA

When my children were very young, they always got new pyjamas on Christmas Eve. I would wrap the pyjamas up and put them on their pillows ready for when they got out of the bath.

Even though my children are now adults, the tradition has continued. They no longer live at home, but they still come back for their 'surprise' Christmas Eve presents and my daughter now does the same for her children.

SONYA

IDEAS FOR AUTUMN TRADITIONS

1. Make a thanksgiving pumpkin by writing things that you're thankful for all over it or carving pictures of things you're thankful for into it

2. Go conker picking, learn how to play conkers and hold a competition

3. Make an autumn wreath using what you can find outside

4. Look for leaves in the garden and make a collage

5. Close the curtains, snuggle up and have a movie night

> My husband and I buy
> one new Christmas bauble every
> year, often from special places we've
> visited. They hold such precious
> memories. We recently lost our baby,
> Holly, and we now have a bauble that
> represents her, which will
> forever hang on our tree.

JESSICA

Each year, around the time that the Queen's New Year Honours list is announced, we write a list of the people in our family and local community that we think deserve to be honoured.

We write them a certificate for each person explaining why we think they deserve a medal and post it through their door!

MILO

We always make two Christmas puddings at the end of November – one for Christmas Day and one that we save until Easter Day. We have a special poem (about a mysterious fairy godmother), that we recite as we stir the mixture, which I have known off by heart since I was little and which my children are now learning too.

This tradition makes me feel connected with my mum and my granny, who taught me to do this. As I help my little ones to stir the mixture as it gets heavier and heavier, I feel so much a part of something bigger that is being passed down through the generations. Repeating the poem is so special to me as it is not only something to treasure from my family's history but equally something that will be passed through future generations too.

The tradition of keeping one pudding back for Easter helps me to be intentional about telling the whole story – that without Christmas we wouldn't have Easter. It's a simple way of remembering to tell one another about how the festivals are linked in this amazing story and it helps us to remember that Christmas is only part of the story – the climax of Easter is still to come. It's important to me because it's a fun way of demonstrating and living out our faith in a natural, food-based way that everyone can engage in.

HANNAH

> Every New Year's Eve my wife and I go out for coffee and talk about the year ahead. We set goals for ourselves individually but also think about things we want to work on as a couple. We also talk about how we're doing spiritually and check things are aligned as they should be. We then also look back at the prior year and talk about what we're thankful for.

STEPHEN

My dad was the king of making traditions out of nothing and loved to invest in us. As a teenager, he made Friday night our special night, where we would play games and cook a special supper together. He showed me how to make toffee, fudge, and homemade crisps, and we would sit down and watch the TV show *Cheers* together. It took me a while to be tempted out with my friends on a Friday as I loved this so much.

I am one of four children, which was quite a challenge for my mum, especially at Christmas when she was trying to do all of the preparations. In order for things to run smoothly, my dad would take me and my sister out (we were much younger than my two older brothers and they could amuse themselves). He sold this 'outing' to us as a special task that we had been given. This last thing to do, after all of the other decorations had been put up was to fetch fresh holly to hang on the pictures around the house. He made us feel so important by entrusting us with this special job, and to this day picking holly still reminds me of him so much.

On our walk to the woods, we would pass through a railway tunnel and he would stand at one end and ask us to close our eyes, for we were going to magically jump over the tunnel, through the sky to the other side. My sister and I grabbed a hand each, both of us fully trusting him as we ran through the tunnel to his shouts of "Don't open your eyes, we are flying!" As we grew older, we naturally realised that this was pretend, but we didn't feel cheated. We just laughed so much at the thought of us believing it was real for a couple of years. He still insisted that we were flying!

After that, we would walk around the woods inspecting each holly bush that we found to see if it was the best. We would then carefully select a branch and Dad would tenderly cut it and place it into the bag, as if it were china. This was something that we looked forward to every year. It was a magical time with my dad and it was part of our family Christmas. When I had my son, I carried on the tradition of walking to some local woods on Christmas Eve to gather holly. I told him that this was something we used to do with Granddad George in the woods where I grew up, and making the finishing touches to Christmas by putting holly on the picture frames has now been passed to another generation.

When my dad was alive, he would visit us over Christmas and would always comment on how lovely the holly-dressed pictures looked, thanking my son for helping to decorate them. My son was even privileged enough to share a Grandad George tunnel jump when he was young! Now that my dad has passed away, we still do it. It's a special part of our Christmas. We remember my dad and tell funny stories about him as we walk and search for holly. It brings his memory into our present.

LIS

IDEAS FOR
AS THE CLOCKS CHANGE

1. Have a sleepover in the living room

2. When we lose an hour, with one hour less to spend cooking, have a takeaway

3. When we gain an hour, choose something special to do with the extra hour

4. Wrap up warm and go stargazing

5. Have a toys clear-out as the seasons change

For the past twenty years I have always made leek and potato soup for Bonfire Night.

KAT

We always wait until after Christmas lunch to open family presents. One year, my husband started wearing all of his gifts and ever since then, the males in the family will wear any clothes they have been given as they are unwrapped – hats, scarves, t-shirts, sweatshirts, even Christmas pants – over whatever they are already wearing!

When my daughter got married, her brother – representing my deceased husband – made a short speech wearing Christmas pants over his suit!

NICOLA

We always celebrate 'name days' which are hugely significant for a lot of Catholic and Orthodox families throughout the world. In Greek culture, name days are really important. Many of us are named after saints and, in fact, for many Greeks, name days are more important than birthdays.

It's customary to congratulate someone on their name day, and so in our family, the day is filled with phone calls from well-wishers! As a family, we have our own tradition of always hosting an open house on our name days. We invite friends, family and neighbours to call in at any point during the day or evening. My dad prepares the most amazing buffet full of traditional Greek food and we celebrate all day.

This is one of my very favourite family traditions and it was started by my grandparents, who've now passed away. Even though they're no longer here, I feel such a connection with them on these name days.

GAVRIELLA

About a decade ago, I heard Rob Parsons speak. He recounted the story of taking his children out in the car in their pyjamas at night, with a torch to look for rabbits, and how it was one of his kids' favourite memories.

We took this idea and created our own tradition of a night time pyjama trip in the car to find the best Christmas lights in Cardiff. As our children got older, they began making their own certificates and posting them through the letterbox of the house that they think has the best lights.

Last year, on a local Facebook page, one of the winners posted a photo of our certificate and said how much it had meant to their family. Thanks Rob for sparking the idea!

SARAH-LOUISE

> "There's nothing I love more than getting up at sunrise on a warm summer's day, walking to the local pier and fishing. While my family are fast asleep, I patiently wait for each fish to take my bait. Once I have enough fish to feed us all, I call my wife who meets me on the beach with our kids and a disposable barbecue. We cook the fish and eat them for breakfast. Barbecued fish for breakfast is fast becoming a favourite tradition of ours!
>
> **BILL**

We always have a family spring clean one weekend in March. We each take responsibility for our own bedrooms and then work together on the other rooms of the house.

We have a massive sort out of all our things, donate toys and clothes that have been outgrown to a local charity and clean the areas of our home that never seem to get done at any time. We work together as a team and always have something special for dinner that night to reward our hard work.

It may sound boring but we actually have a lot of fun doing this together and it brings with it a great sense of achievement.

EMMA

IDEAS FOR DECEMBER TRADITIONS

1. Watch a nativity film while decorating the house

2. Make fudge or cookies together and deliver them to family and friends

3. Complete an act of kindness every day for thirty-one days

4. Make your own advent calendars

5. Join a local Boxing Day swim in the sea (or do your own as a family!)

> One of my most favourite traditions is having homemade chips to eat on Boxing Day. Not only do they taste better than all of the other chips in the world, but it's about family and being together.
>
> My mum loves to feed people and so seeing her three boys devouring HER homemade chips brings a huge smile to her face! But the tradition runs deeper than that; my grandad (mum's dad) would constantly talk about his Boxing Day chips and how he actually preferred them to a Christmas dinner.
>
> This tradition keeps his memory alive and brings comfort to my mum. Good ol' Len – thanks for the chips!
>
> MATTHEW

Use these pages to write or draw your own traditions.

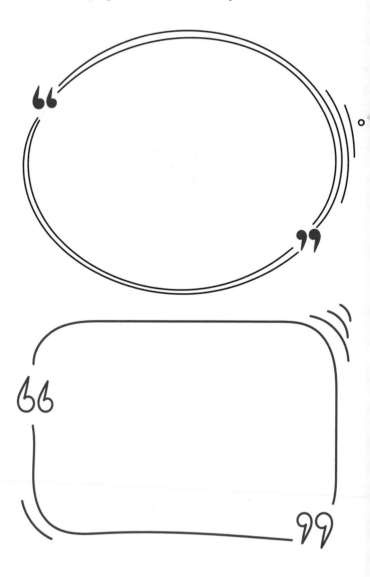

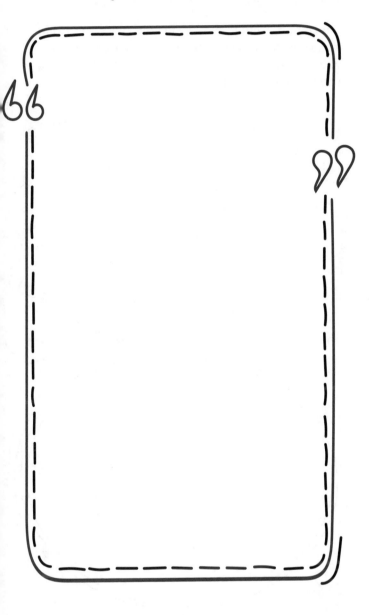

These pages are for you to fill with your memories. You may wish to use the space to write or draw your memories or stick in photos or memorabilia – the choice is yours!

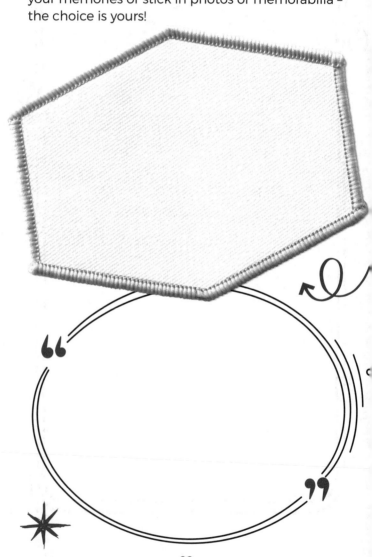

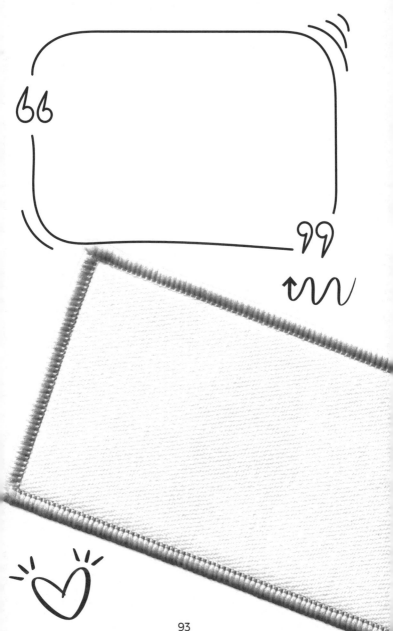

TRADITIONS FOR MILESTONES

What is a milestone? I wonder if the milestones you celebrate with your family are similar to ours? We all place value on different things in life and so it shouldn't come as a surprise that we choose to celebrate different things. What your family counts as a milestone may be something that would pass us by in an instant, and what we choose to celebrate may feel completely alien to your family. But that's the beauty of traditions – they are personal to us.

Milestones are key moments in our lives when we pause to mark a particular point in life, or to celebrate an achievement. Let's take graduating from university or college as an example. After many years of studying and putting all that you've learnt into practice, you are finally qualified in your chosen field. To mark this occasion and all that you've achieved, most universities and colleges will host a graduation ceremony for graduates and loved ones, where these achievements are publicly recognised and applauded. In that moment, the milestone is marked, creating memories that will be looked back on for many years to come. The milestones that you traditionally celebrate as a family could include a baby's christening or dedication, first and last days of school, the first time someone rides a roller-coaster, getting your first job, learning a new skill, passing an exam, securing a place on a sports team and anything else that you'd like. There are no rules when it comes to the milestones that you celebrate. What's key is that they're important to your family.

As with other traditions, celebrating milestones can play a meaningful part of family life without needing to be big or expensive. Some of the best memories can come from things that cost very little and having a variety of traditions that differ in cost, time and preparation can be key to keeping things fun and enjoyable for all.

Milestones cause us to stop and celebrate. When looking back in years to come, we'll not only remember our achievements, big and small, but also how we intentionally chose to celebrate them. Choosing to have traditions that mark milestones can help to create these powerful memories that we will look back on with fondness. So when a milestone gives you the opportunity to shout to all the world, "I made it to this point! Let's celebrate!" why not gather your family or friends and make some memories together?

Every year we buy
each other anniversary gifts that
traditionally match the number of years
that we've been married, for example
paper for first year, cotton for the second
year, leather for the third year, etc. Some
are easier than others to do and we
always choose to get creative
in our gift giving.

ZOE

> On birthdays, the other siblings in the family would always have an 'unbirthday' gift. This meant that you were given a gift because it wasn't your birthday!
>
> They were never extravagant gifts – they were mostly small gifts like a book, DVD or a bath bomb – but it meant that you always really looked forward to your siblings' birthday, as you knew you'd get a gift too! We loved having a tradition that felt unique to our family!
>
> BECKY

As children, we had the most wonderful tradition that still brings a smile to my face.

On our birthdays we were allowed to choose the tie that our dad would wear for work. My dad had to leave for work early but he always took the time to make us feel special before he had to go. It didn't matter to him how his outfit looked (he had a lot of wacky ties to choose from!) and we knew that he would spend the day proudly telling people that he was wearing that specific tie because it was one of his children's birthday. It was his way of showing us that our birthdays were the most important things to him, while he was at work as well as when he was at home.

He also gave the birthday child a piggyback down the stairs to breakfast, which only ever happened on a birthday!

HANNAH

In our family, when someone finishes school, we frame the shirt or t-shirt that their friends have signed and put it on the wall!

JUDY

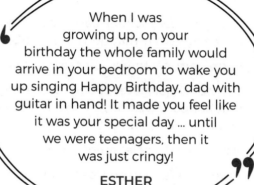

When I was growing up, on your birthday the whole family would arrive in your bedroom to wake you up singing Happy Birthday, dad with guitar in hand! It made you feel like it was your special day ... until we were teenagers, then it was just cringy!

ESTHER

IDEAS FOR INVOLVING SCHOOL LEAVERS

1. Hold your own school leavers ceremony online for family that don't live nearby

2. Write personal thank you cards to teachers

3. Let the school leaver choose everything that happens that day, for example wake up time, meals and activities

4. Have a special celebration meal

5. Have close family members (or friends) write down something that they love and admire about the school leaver and have them read each of the affirmations aloud

66

We always celebrate exams with a treat before the results come in. We intentionally choose to celebrate the effort, not the achievement.

LAWRENCE

99

"
When I was growing up,
we had a birthday compliments jar.
On the eve of someone's birthday,
we would all write down one thing
that we loved about that person and
place it in the jar. Then the following
morning, the birthday girl or
boy would read aloud their
compliments.

NOEL

"

We acquired a 'birthday box' a few years ago and it's become a birthday tradition of ours. It's well used and getting a bit worse for wear in some places but each birthday it comes out and all of the wrapped presents are placed inside it.

On the eve of a birthday, we put it in our bedroom, complete with the number of balloons for whatever age the birthday boy or girl is turning. In the morning, the kids pile onto our bed, the birthday child in pride of place, while their siblings give them the presents from the box one by one. The birthday child points to which present they'd like next and their siblings deliver it to them.

They still love it even though the boys are now teenagers!

TIM

> Every year, around the time of our wedding anniversary, we go for dinner at our wedding venue, which happens to be a restaurant. It's always such a special night for us.

MATTHEW

> Our first son very sadly died the day after he was born. Ever since, we have had a tradition where we always make a cake for his birthday and sing 'Happy Birthday' to him. His brothers have grown up doing this and are still happy to do it even though they are now in their late teens and early twenties. It means a lot to us as a family.
>
> LISA

I'm married to a British-Ghanaian man and we have three daughters. It's so wonderful to be able to not only learn about Ghanaian customs and traditions but to pass them on to our children.

One tradition that we've intentionally chosen to continue is to give our children a Ghanaian middle name, which is unique to the day of the week that they are born on. For example, our eldest daughter was born on a Sunday, giving her the middle name Akosia. Our second daughter has the middle name Afia, as she was born on a Friday. Our third daughter has the middle name Nana-Akosua, which is an alternative name for a girl born on a Sunday.

It's really important to us that we pass these customs and traditions on to our children as it's an integral part of who they are. I hope that this, and many other traditions, are passed on through our children for generations to come.

IRENE

IDEAS FOR ANNIVERSARY TRADITIONS

1. Take a trip down memory lane – reminisce about your favourite memories

2. Do something special to remember someone who has died

3. Make a playlist of your favourite songs as a couple or family

4. Make a toast to someone's memory

5. Reflect on the year that passed and dream for the year to come

In our family, we have a tradition whereby we club together and buy car-related gifts for the person who has just passed their driving test. Previous gifts have included novelty car mats, steering-wheel covers, scatter cushions, air fresheners and bumper stickers!

They're a bit of fun and help bring a uniqueness to their first car. It's a tradition that has been passed down through the generations in my family and is always a laugh.

JAKE

> We always do a special
> birthday breakfast for each
> member of the family. The night before,
> we decorate the kitchen with balloons,
> lay the table with our 'birthday tablecloth'
> and put out all the presents and cards.
> We make fresh orange juice in the
> morning and prepare the birthday
> person's favourite breakfast
> to 'surprise' them!

KATE

A few years ago, my husband was working nights on my birthday and therefore wasn't going to be there when I woke up. Before he went to work the night before, he decorated the house, including buying and putting up some 'Happy Birthday' bunting for me.

We've had the bunting ever since and it gets put up the night before anyone in our family has a birthday, ready for them to come downstairs to in the morning. It's now getting a bit dog-eared in places, but it's the birthday bunting and it wouldn't be the same if we replaced it!

KEREN

> We take our children's first day of school photos in the exact same place every single year. It's so lovely to look back and see them growing up and changing.

CATHRYN

> In our family, we love celebrating 'half birthdays', exactly six months after each birthday. We celebrate that person by choosing a small gift for them and by giving them the honour of deciding the meal that we will all eat together. It's such a unique tradition – we don't know anyone else who celebrates half birthdays – and that adds to the joy of the day!

CERYS

IDEAS FOR TRADITIONS DURING EXAM SEASON

1. Run a special bubble bath for your child the night before an exam

2. Have some one-to-one time with your child to talk about any exam worries or fears

3. Reward effort, rather than just success

4. Put a note in their lunch box or pencil case reminding them how proud you are of them

5. Have their favourite dessert ready to eat after an exam

We always celebrate a family member's new job with a cake.

TANYA

We always have funerals for our pets. We each say something that we loved about them and then we bury them with their favourite food. This might sound a little morbid to some people, but as children it helped us to process what had happened and to remember them fondly.

SUE

The traditional wedding anniversary gift for the first year of marriage is paper, so my husband and I decided to make this a love letter. It was such a wonderful thing that we vowed to do this every year. This love letter is one of the highlights of the year and we've not failed to give our letters for thirteen years.

This tradition reminds us of the love we have for each other and is specific in highlighting those things that we love about each other. The letters encourage us, and build confidence and gratitude in our relationship.

LESLEY

> We mark the cat's birthday – he always gets a card!
>
> **EMILY**

I grew up in a culture where naming ceremonies were the norm. In Nigerian culture, when you have a baby you're given seven days to name them. On the seventh day after the baby's birth, a naming ceremony takes place where friends and family gather together. There is lots of food, celebrations galore, the baby's names are announced and prayers are said. It is such a special day and a tradition that is really treasured.

While we don't live in Nigeria and our son isn't being brought up around a lot of Nigerian culture, it's still really important to me that I'm able to pass on traditions and customs from my heritage to him.

DANIELLA

My sister-in-law has started a new birthday tradition on our family WhatsApp group. She and my brother have three little ones and they will always get the older two kids to sing Happy Birthday to the grandparent/aunt/uncle whose birthday it is. It's so lovely to get these cute little videos of your niece and nephew singing to you on your birthday!

SARAH R

IDEAS FOR TRADITIONS TO REMEMBER SOMEONE WHO HAS DIED

1. Cook one of their favourite meals

2. Look through photo albums on dates that are special to you

3. Recount stories about them to generations that have come since, as well as those that remember them

4. Light a candle in their memory

5. Visit a favourite place of theirs, or somewhere special that reminds you of them

"We have a favourite tradition that we still do today. When it's someone's birthday we make a cake, invite the family and use my granny's now vintage tea cups and saucers, tiny plates, sugar bowl, tea pots and table cloth and sit at the table together.

These tea parties remind me of my grandparents and how we always celebrated birthdays with them in this way. My children enjoy it and it makes the birthday person feel special. Our extended family love it too and invitations are always accepted!"

CAMILLA

Use these pages to write or draw your own traditions.

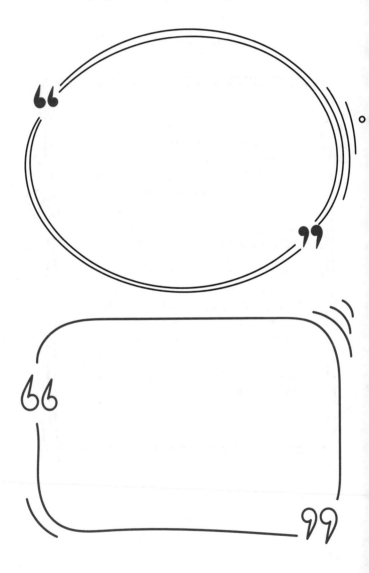

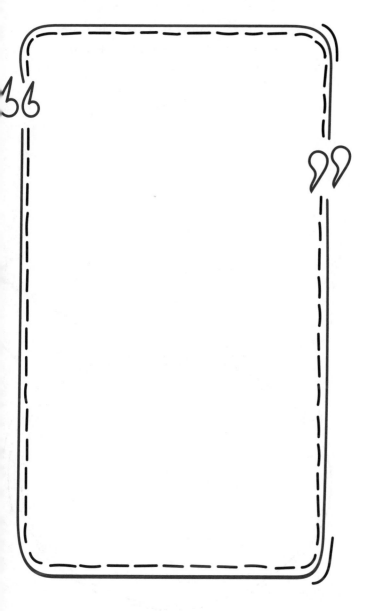

These pages are for you to fill with your memories. You may wish to use the space to write or draw your memories or stick in photos or memorabilia – the choice is yours!

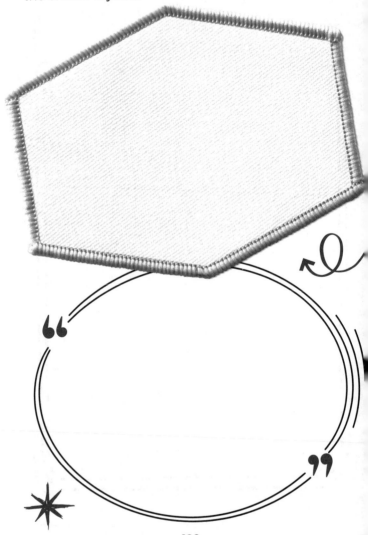

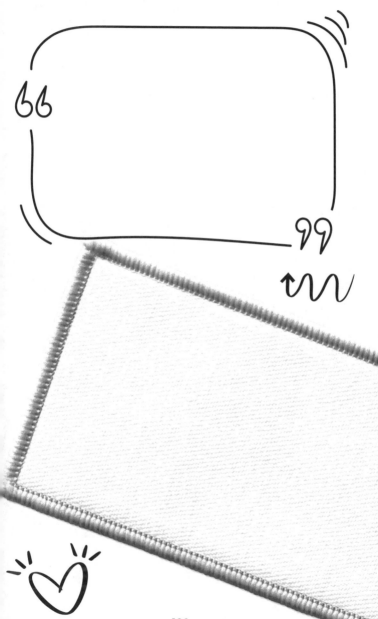

TRADITIONS ON HOLIDAY

What is it that makes a holiday a holiday? What special ingredient is added that makes these times just that little bit sweeter? We would say that a holiday is simply any amount of time that you set aside to do something special, or to go somewhere different. It's a chance to get away from the regular day-to-day activities and instead do things that you choose to do.

With that in mind, a holiday could be a few days away from work or school to have a camping adventure, time spent taking in the richness of another culture abroad, or anything and everything else you can imagine!

Holidays can also bring with them the chance for quality time spent with extended family and friends. Memories can be made with grandparents, cousins, childhood friends, and everyone in between! While the distance between us and our friends and family can be a barrier in connecting during an ordinary week, holidays can help us overcome that. These times give us the opportunity for longer car journeys, late nights spent catching up and maybe even people to share our home with for a little while. Holidays lend themselves well to a sense of adventure, the change in pace giving a chance to explore and imagine. What was ordinary to us in everyday life can seem almost magical in these slower-paced times. Holidays are a great opportunity to take part in different customs and traditions, and maybe even start some new ones too.

"

My uncle and auntie live by the coast and during the school holidays my grandparents would take my brother and I to stay there. We would always go when the regatta was on and breakfast on the pier became a favourite tradition of mine.

My wonderful grandmother has since passed away, but every time we visit my uncle and auntie we make sure that we go for breakfast on that same pier, make a toast to them with our coffees and orange juices, and recount our stories of memories made with them – a new tradition born out of an old one.

ADAM

"

> We always create a summer holiday bucket list and try to do everything on the list before the first day back at school.
>
> **ROSA**

Once a year, during the holidays, we would all pile into the car and take it in turns to give driving instructions to my dad. We had no idea where we were going; we would just tell him to turn either left or right at every junction, as well as letting him know which exit to take at each roundabout.

Once we were happy with where we had found ourselves, we would stop and have a day to explore this new place. Often, we would only end up a few miles from our house but it always felt like such an adventure!

ELAINE

> We always have Jaffa cakes and Welsh cakes in the car while travelling on holidays.
>
> **LUCIE**

" We always buy a fridge magnet from the places we've visited on holiday. Over the past thirty years we have collected what must be hundreds. Every now and again I take a moment to stand in front of our fridge and recall the memories that we've made.

ELLIE "

I'm originally from Spain and every year during the summer holidays we have what we call a 'Spain day' as a family. It only ever happens during the summer holidays – never at any other time – and that seems to add to the excitement of the day. I cook traditional Spanish food and we watch Spanish cartoons and films together.

Our children, born in the UK, love to hear stories of my childhood spent in Spain and the mischief that I used to get up to with my siblings! One year, our youngest daughter asked to decorate the house, and since then Spanish-themed decorations have become an integral part of 'Spain day'! Our children love this day so much that they've now started asking to invite their friends!

For us as parents, it's a really special way of teaching our children about their heritage as well as making precious memories as a family.

ISABELLA

IDEAS FOR SUNNY DAYS IN THE SUMMER HOLIDAYS

1. Catch an early morning sunrise

2. Make your own lollipops

3. Have a water fight

4. Hold your own sports day and invite some friends

5. Have breakfast in the garden

I only ever read books on holiday and every holiday I buy a new book. If I buy one at another point in the year, I know that it won't get read until I'm on holiday.

LUKE J

On family holidays we would collect as many leaflets as possible about all of the attractions in the local area before coming together for a family meeting. During this meeting, each of us children could request one thing we wanted to do. We would then plan the week so everyone had a chance to do their choice of activity.

CAMILLA

> When I was a child, we lived in lots of different countries. My grandpa, part-owned a second house in his street, and we used to stay in it when we went back to the UK for summer holidays.
>
> Some of my siblings and I used to get up early and run over the neighbour's front lawns (usually barefoot!) to my grandpa's house, where we'd have boiled eggs and soldiers with him. Usually he'd have my aunt's Dalmatian in the kitchen with him, as he dog-sat while she was at work, and part of the fun was trying to keep the dog from eating your breakfast.

SARAH-NAOMI

EGG & SOLDIERS · WITH GRANDPARENTS ·

We were always allowed a second helping of ice cream during the summer holidays, but not at any other time!

JADE

My grandparents
used to take us on trips
to the seaside during the school
holidays. We would always choose
one special shell to take home with
us. I still have some of those shells
and they bring such a smile to
my face as I remember my
wonderful grandparents.

JOSHUA

IDEAS FOR STAYCATION TRADITIONS

1. Design your own passports and tickets

2. Be a tourist in your own community and do some things that you wouldn't normally do

3. Turn your house into your own personal hotel or restaurant

4. Have a day trip with another family

5. Go camping in your own garden

> We always take small individual cereal boxes with us on holiday. It's the only time of year that we have them.

BECKY

" Whenever we visit a country where English is not the main spoken language we pick ten new words and five new phrases to learn in the native language of that country. We then try and make sure that we've said all of these things by the time we go home – like a game of language bingo! "

AMY

Growing up, we would always host our very own summer Olympics. We took it incredibly seriously and put a huge amount of planning into this special day. Extended family and friends were invited and each of us represented a different country.

Our 'Olympic sports' were activities such as bean bag tossing, water balloon throwing, hula hooping, running 100 metres and skipping rope jumping. We would have homemade Olympic themed snacks and even host our own opening and closing ceremonies, complete with certificates and prizes for the winners.

This became an annual tradition in our house and was well known among our friends. Looking back, I can't believe the commitment and effort that my mum put in every single year to make the day such a success. My siblings and I are now all in our thirties and we still reminisce about it.

JENNA

When I was a child, our annual summer bank holiday football tournament and picnic was a firm favourite of mine.

Around thirty of us would gather together on this day for food and fun. There was always such a great atmosphere and a real sense of community. Our time together would last as long as we wanted it to – there was never a rush to finish the day.

Looking back, those days always seemed sunny and they made for great memories.

IMA

"During the summer holidays we always go to a particular quiet cove we knew with fewer tourists, and build sandcastles and wait for the tide to come in. We'd then 'defend' the sandcastle against the incoming waves by building flood defences out of sand.

NAOMI"

We always do a 'treat-swap' during the school holidays as most of my extended family still live in Sweden.

About three to four times a year, always during the holidays, my children and my sister's children cram as many treats (chocolate, sweets and other snacks) into a box and send them to each other! My children receive a box full of Swedish goodies to try and my nieces and nephews get a box full of British ones.

It's such a simple idea, but something that has become a much-loved tradition in our family. It also helps to keep our children connected as we don't get to see each other in person very often.

MARCUS

IDEAS FOR HOLIDAY TRADITIONS TO SHARE WITH EXTENDED FAMILY

1. Start a family book club where you all read the same book and then discuss in person or online

2. Write a letter to a family member who lives far away

3. Do a house swap for one night every half term

4. Host Sunday afternoon tea once every Easter Sunday

5. Set up a family WhatsApp group with extended family members. During half term weeks, each family member sends a daily photo of what they've been doing that day

> We would always choose summer holiday activities by throwing a dart at a dartboard. Each section of the dartboard has a different activity written on it and wherever the dart landed dictated the next activity!

LYNNE

Whenever my cousins
used to come to stay during
the summer holidays we would always
go on an adventure to a particular castle
near where we lived. My grandma would
make us a massive picnic and we would
sit in the same field every year to eat it.
The same food would be eaten in the
grounds of the same castle year after
year and yet it was always
a holiday highlight.

EMMA

Every year we go camping for a week in the summer holidays. Each year we pick a different part of Britain to visit. We always take the same (now old!) beautiful bell tent and all our camping gear, and sleep in one space together.

I always take the same big brown blanket to cover the ground mat (which is put away for the rest of the year!). We toast marshmallows over the firepit in the evening and make 'smores' by sandwiching the marshmallows between chocolate digestives.

KATE

> Every morning while we're on holiday, we each eat a Cadbury's Freddo bar. We call them 'Breakfast Freddos' and they can only be eaten when we are physically away on holiday as a family.

SARA

"When I was a kid, we somehow acquired a baseball hat with a seagull pictured on it. We named it 'The seagull hat'. If someone had their food stolen by a seagull while eating by the seaside, they would have to wear the seagull hat for the rest of the day!"

BILL

IDEAS FOR RAINY DAY TRADITIONS DURING THE SUMMER HOLIDAYS

1. Make an indoor den
2. Complete a jigsaw together
3. Spend an afternoon baking and deliver some baked goods to your neighbours
4. Go puddle jumping
5. Spend two minutes in the rain and see who can then wring the most water out of their clothes

Every year, a local newspaper would run a giveaway for tickets to the local theme park. My mum would buy the newspaper every day that the promotion was running, cut out the tokens that she needed and send away for the tickets. The three of us would then have a special family trip during the summer holidays.

We would leave the house as early as possible to make sure that we were there as soon as the theme park opened. I remember thinking that my mum was fearless as she took us on as many rides as was physically possible, even the ones that made me feel like my stomach was in my mouth!

We would always stay until the park closed when we were asked to leave. This was such a special day and something that we would look forward to every year.

ADAM

Use these pages to write or draw your own traditions.

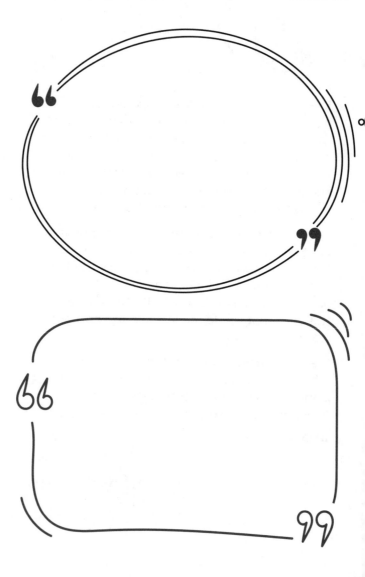

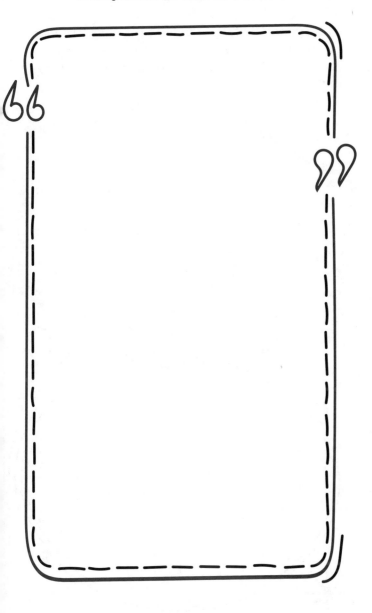

These pages are for you to fill with your memories. You may wish to use the space to write or draw your memories or stick in photos or memorabilia – the choice is yours!

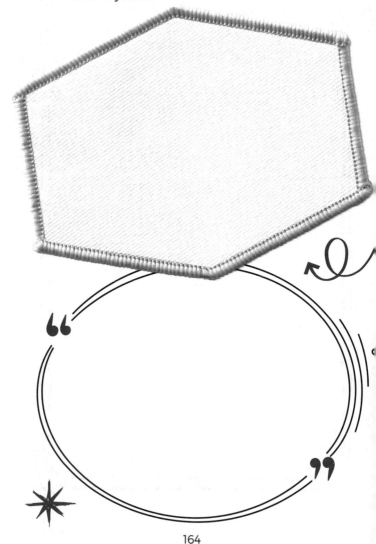

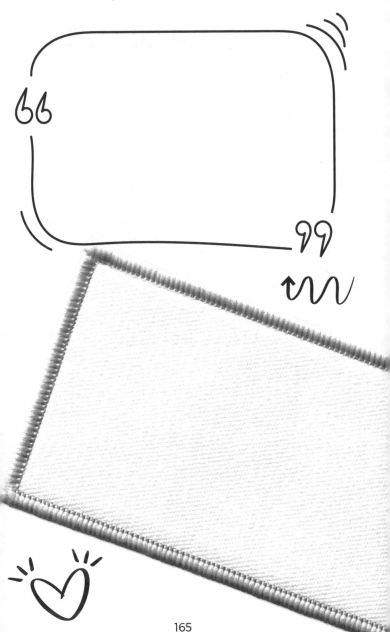

ABOUT CARE FOR THE FAMILY

Care for the Family is a national charity which aims to strengthen family life and help those who face family difficulties. Our work has been focused on the UK, but we are increasingly reaching a wider audience through digital technology.

We focus primarily on the following areas of family life: marriage/couple relationships, parenting and bereavement. Our aim is to be accessible to every family, whatever their circumstances, to provide support in difficult family situations and to create resources that are preventative, evidence-based and easy to apply.

You can keep in touch by subscribing to our newsletter or following us on social media